DyslexiaGames.com

Series B
Book 1

BRAIN FOOD

Art Games, Puzzles & Mystery Patterns

30 Fun Lessons

**Intriguing Mind Games
That Sharpen the Skills
Necessary for Success
in Reading, Writing & Math.**

The Thinking Tree

www.DyslexiaGames.com

Copyright © 2011 the Thinking Tree, LLC
All rights reserved.

Dyslexia Games Series B – Book 1
Friendly Copyright Notice:

ALL DYSLEXIA GAMES, WORKSHEETS, AND MATERIALS MAY <u>NOT</u> BE SHARED, COPIED, EMAILED, OR OTHERWISE DISTRIBUTED TO ANYONE OUTSIDE YOUR HOUSEHOLD OR IMMEDIATE FAMILY (SHARING IS STEALING).

Please refer people interested in Dyslexia Games to our website to purchase their own copy of the materials.

The Thinking Tree LLC • 617 N Swope St. • Greenfield, IN 46140 • info@dyslexiagames.com • +1 (317) 622-8852

BRAIN FOOD
Art Games, Puzzles & Mystery Patterns

By Sarah J. Brown

Parent Teacher Instructions:

Provide the student with a fine point black pen.

Read the instructions on the first four pages to the student. After introducing the child to the first few lessons he should be able to complete the lessons on his own.

These exercises develop symbol recognition, tracking skills, thinking skills, and writing skills.

Draw in the missing parts of each pattern:

Name:_____ Date:_____

© 2011 all rights reserved. The Thinking Tree, LLC

Draw in the missing parts of each picture to make them match the first one:

Name:_____ **Date:**_____

© 2011 all rights reserved. The Thinking Tree, LLC

Draw in the missing parts to compete each letter:

Name:_____ Date:_____

© 2011 all rights reserved. The Thinking Tree, LLC

Name:_____ Date:_____

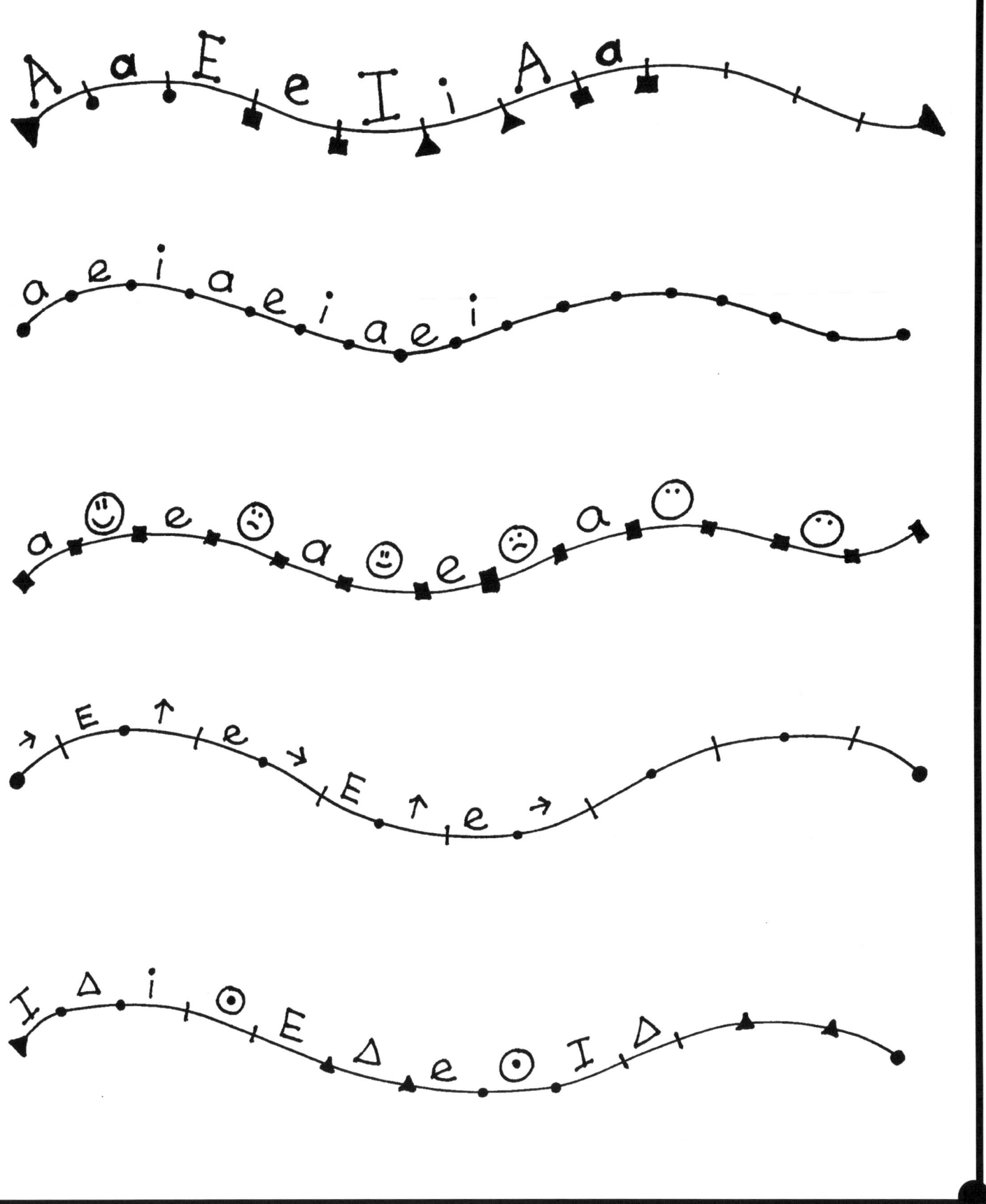

Name:_____ **Date:**_____

© 2011 all rights reserved. The Thinking Tree, LLC

Name:_____ Date:_____

Name:_____ Date:_____

© 2011 all rights reserved. The Thinking Tree, LLC

Name:_____ Date:_____

© 2011 all rights reserved. The Thinking Tree, LLC

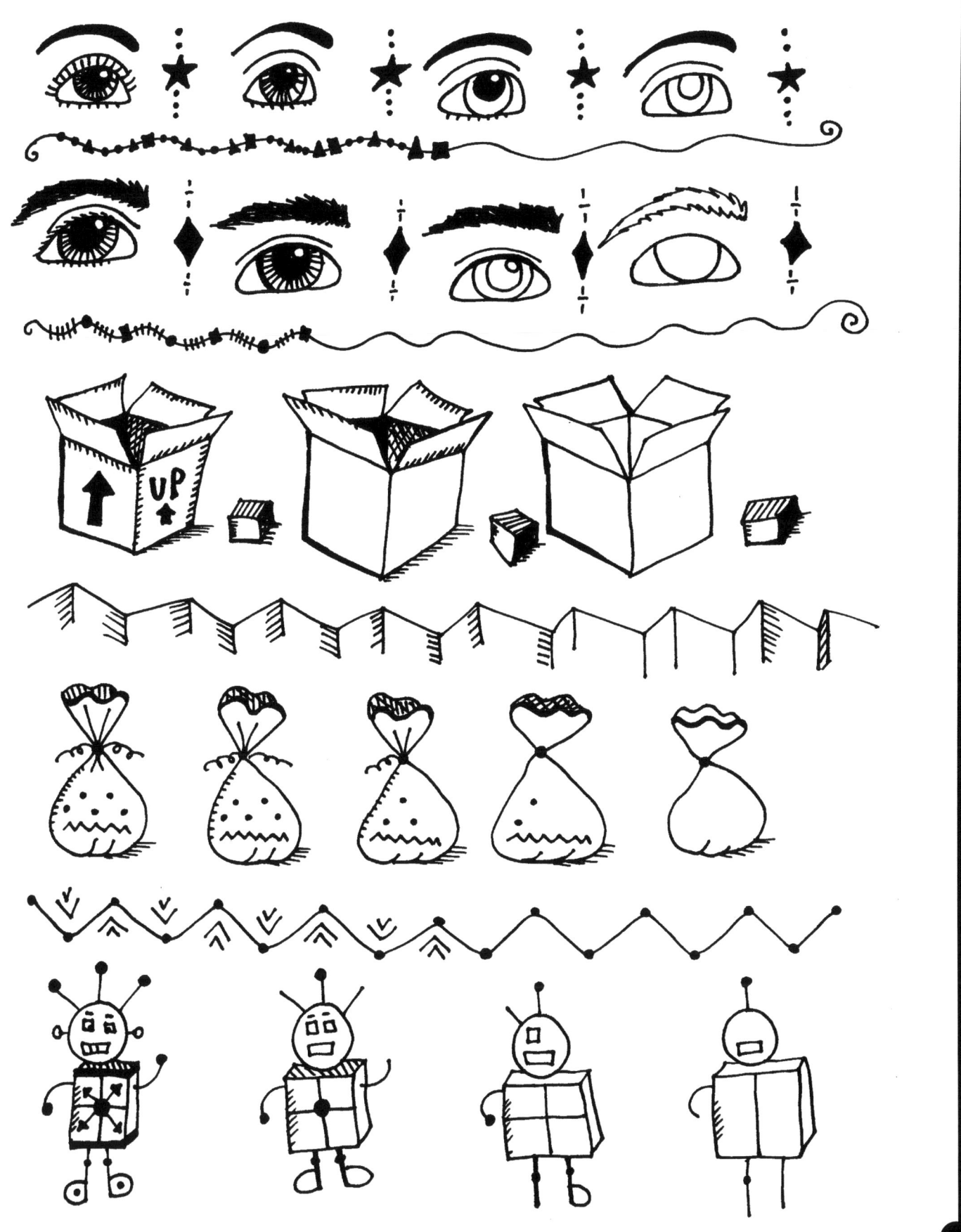

Name:_____ Date:_____

© 2011 all rights reserved. The Thinking Tree, LLC

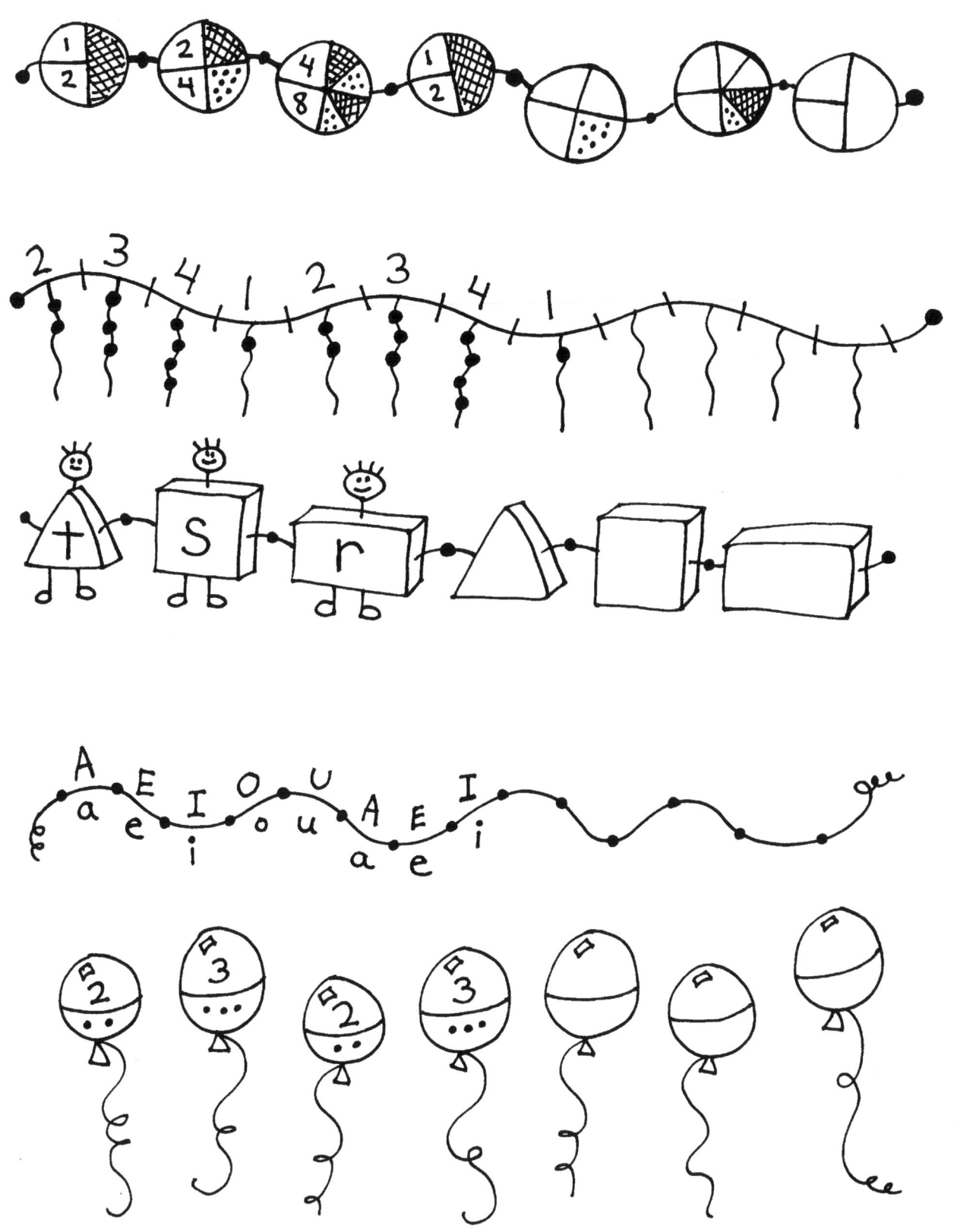

Name:_____   Date:_____

© 2011 all rights reserved. The Thinking Tree, LLC

Name:_____ Date:_____

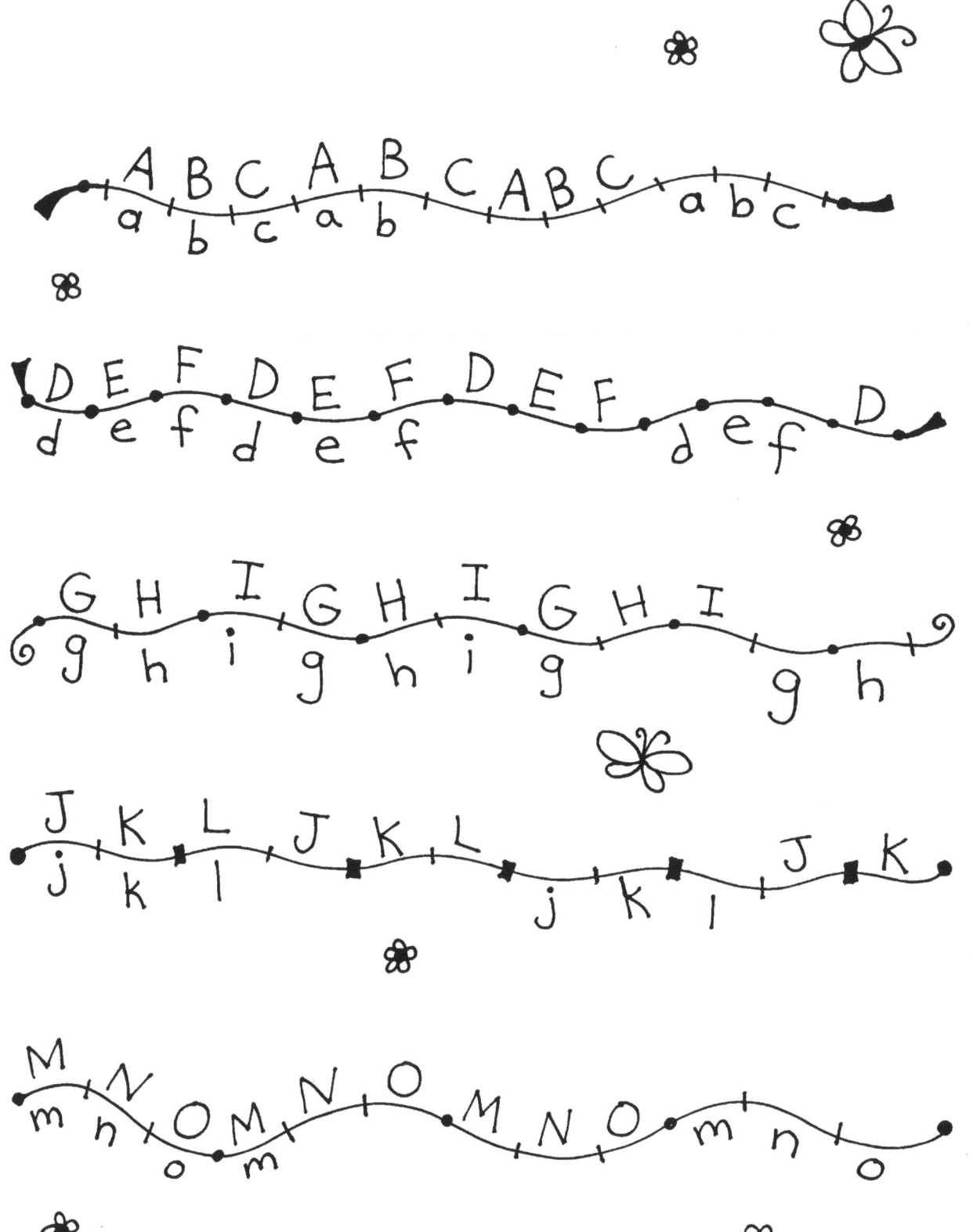

Name:_____ Date:_____

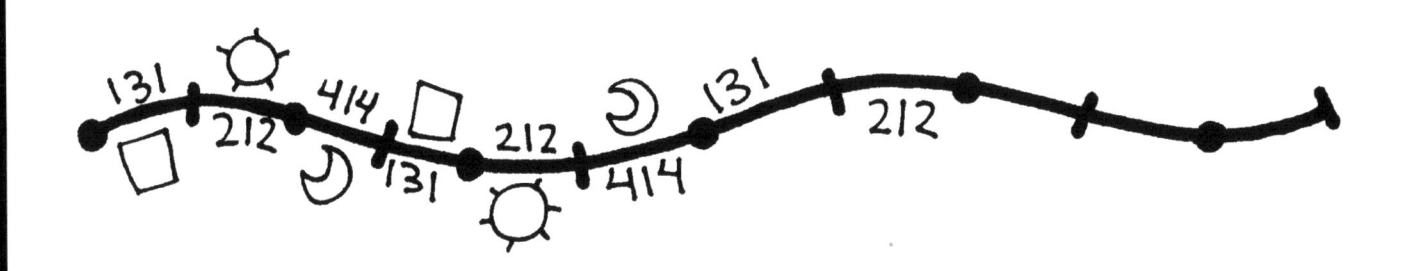

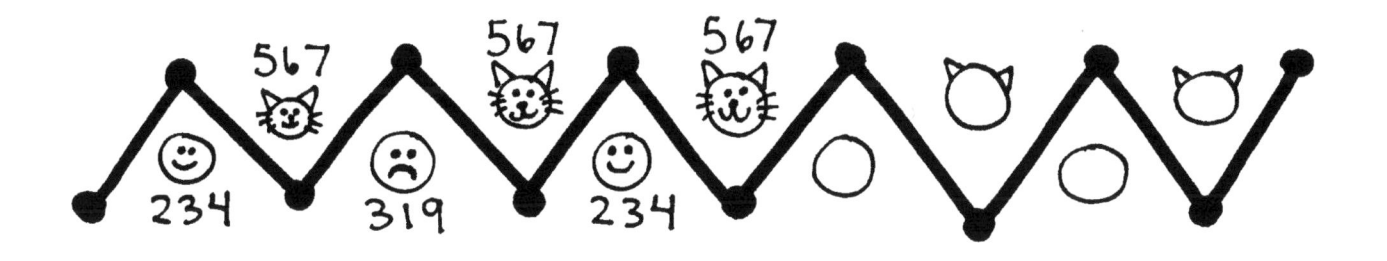

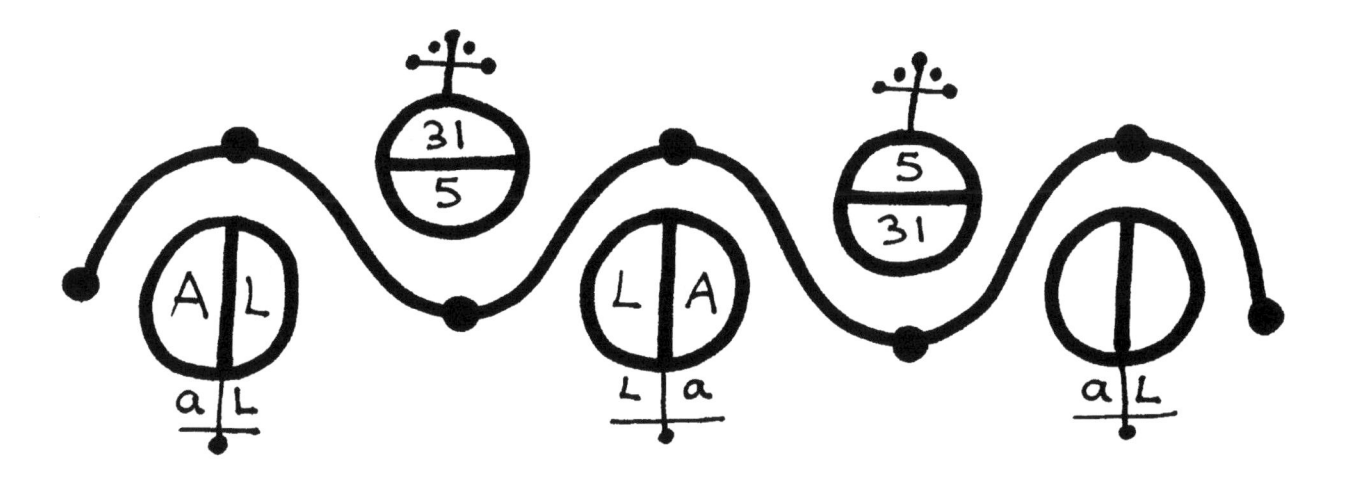

Name: _____ **Date:** _____

© 2011 all rights reserved. The Thinking Tree, LLC

Name:_____ Date:_____

Name: _____ Date: _____

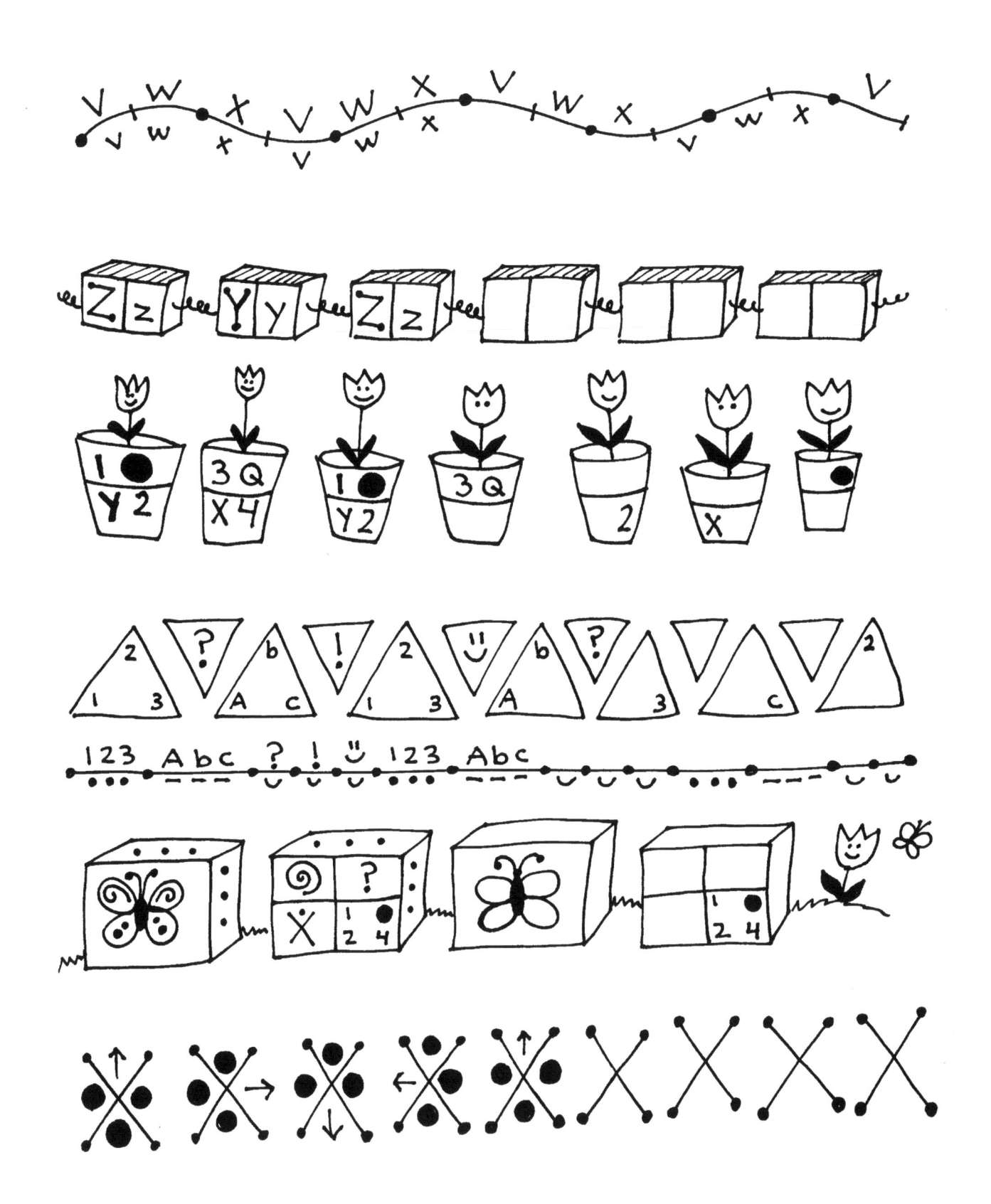

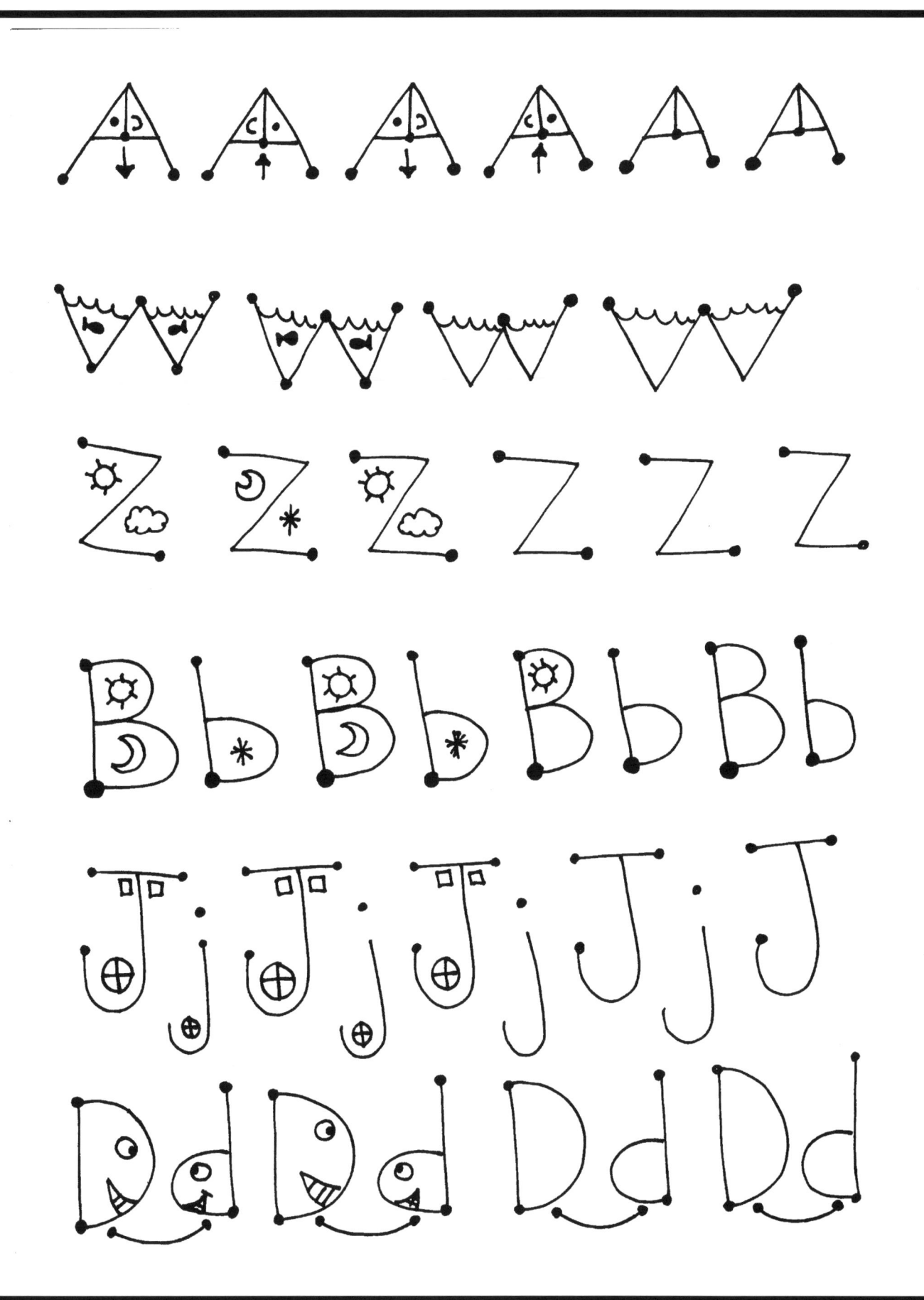

Name:_____ Date:_____

© 2011 all rights reserved. The Thinking Tree, LLC

AaBbCc A_ B_ C_ A_

Name:_____ Date:_____

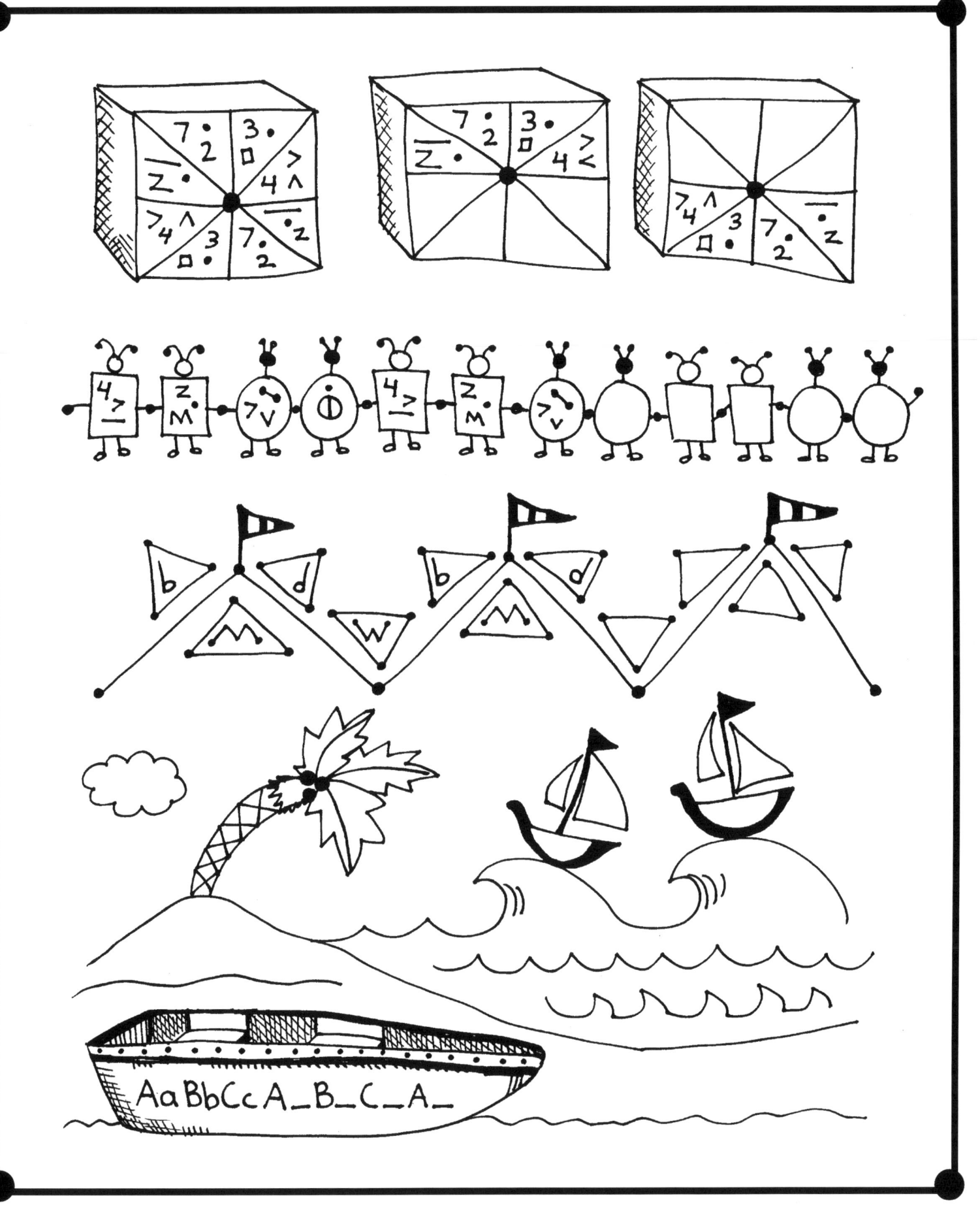

© 2011 all rights reserved. The Thinking Tree, LLC

Name:_____ Date:_____

© 2011 all rights reserved. The Thinking Tree, LLC

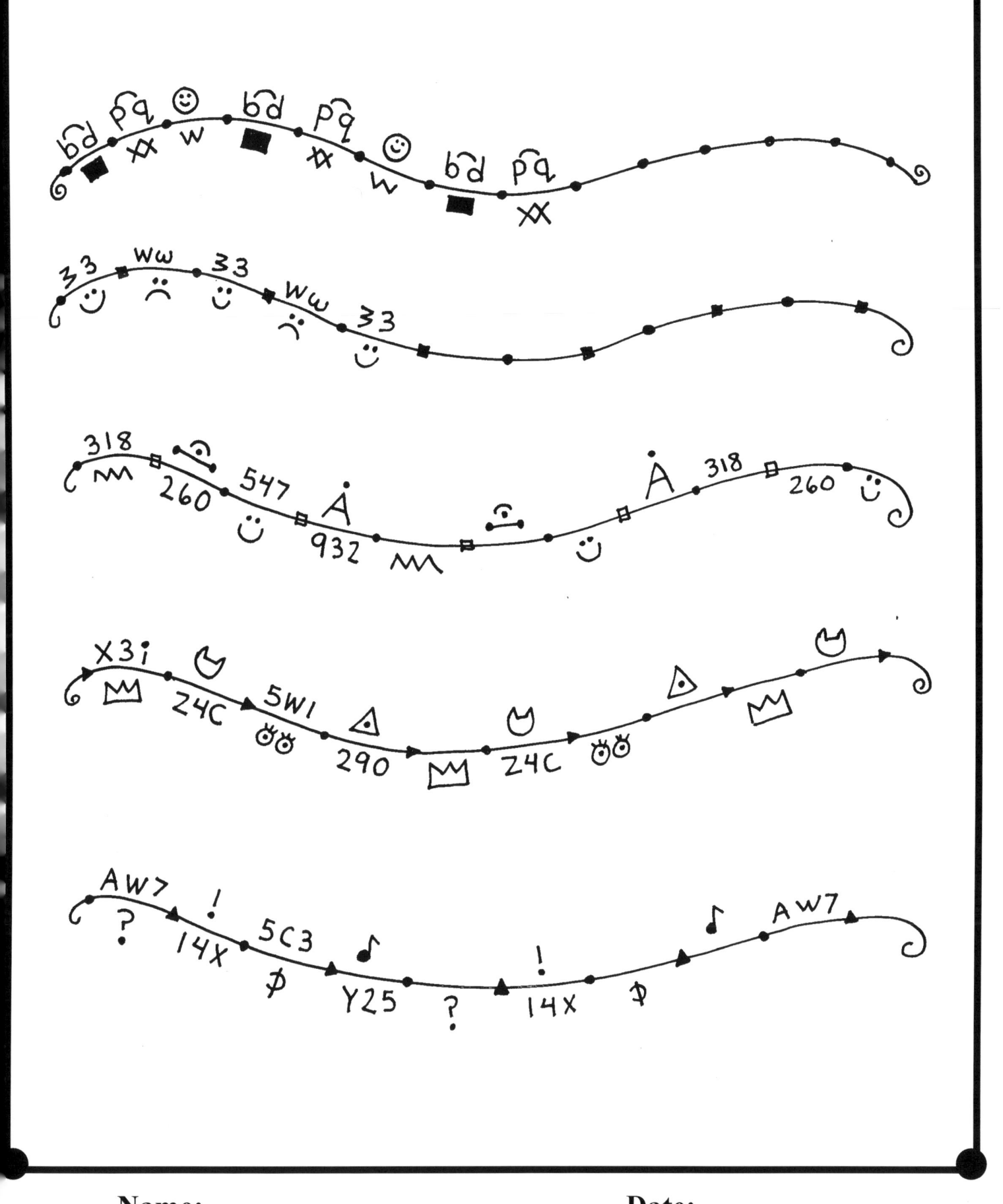

Name:_____ Date:_____

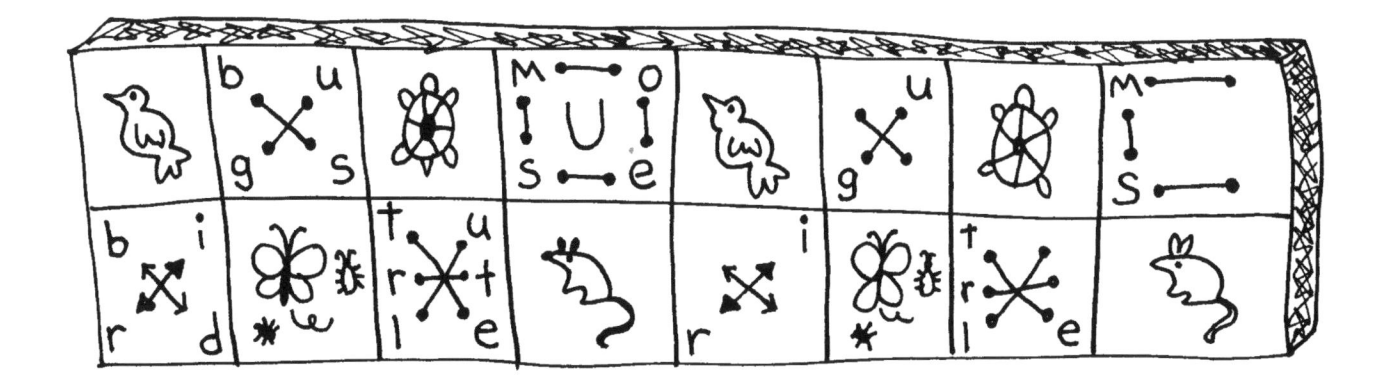

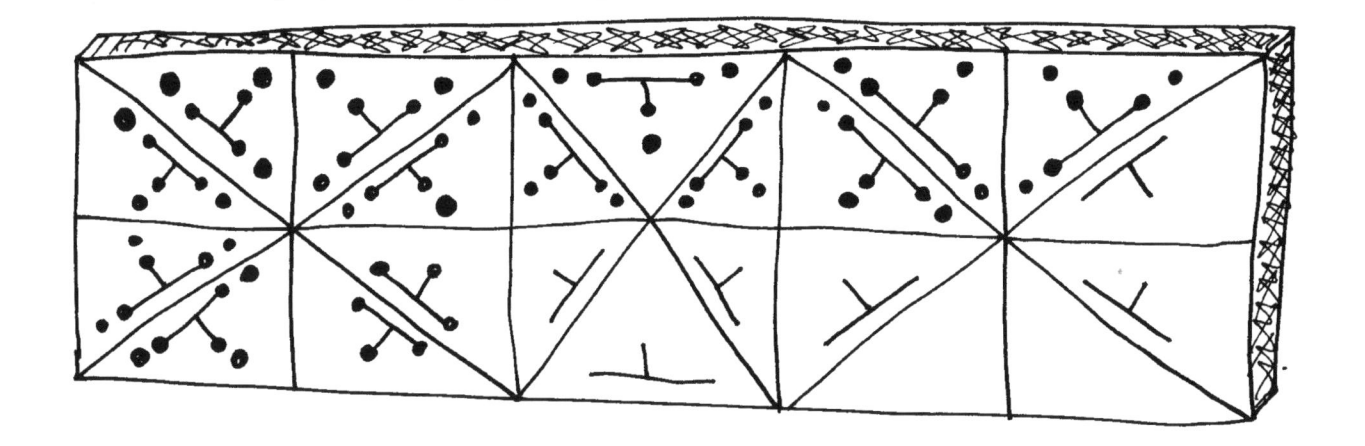

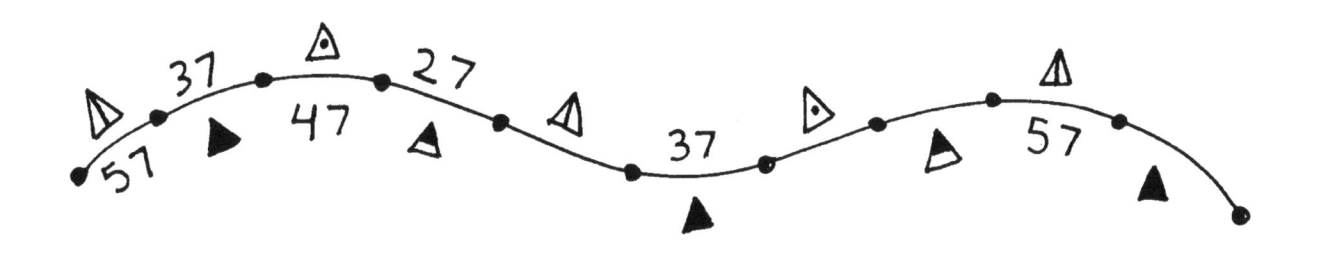

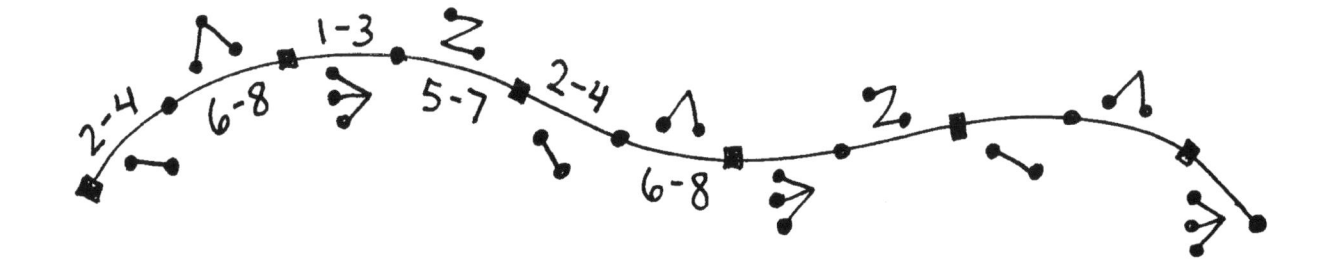

Name:_____ Date:_____

© 2011 all rights reserved. The Thinking Tree, LLC

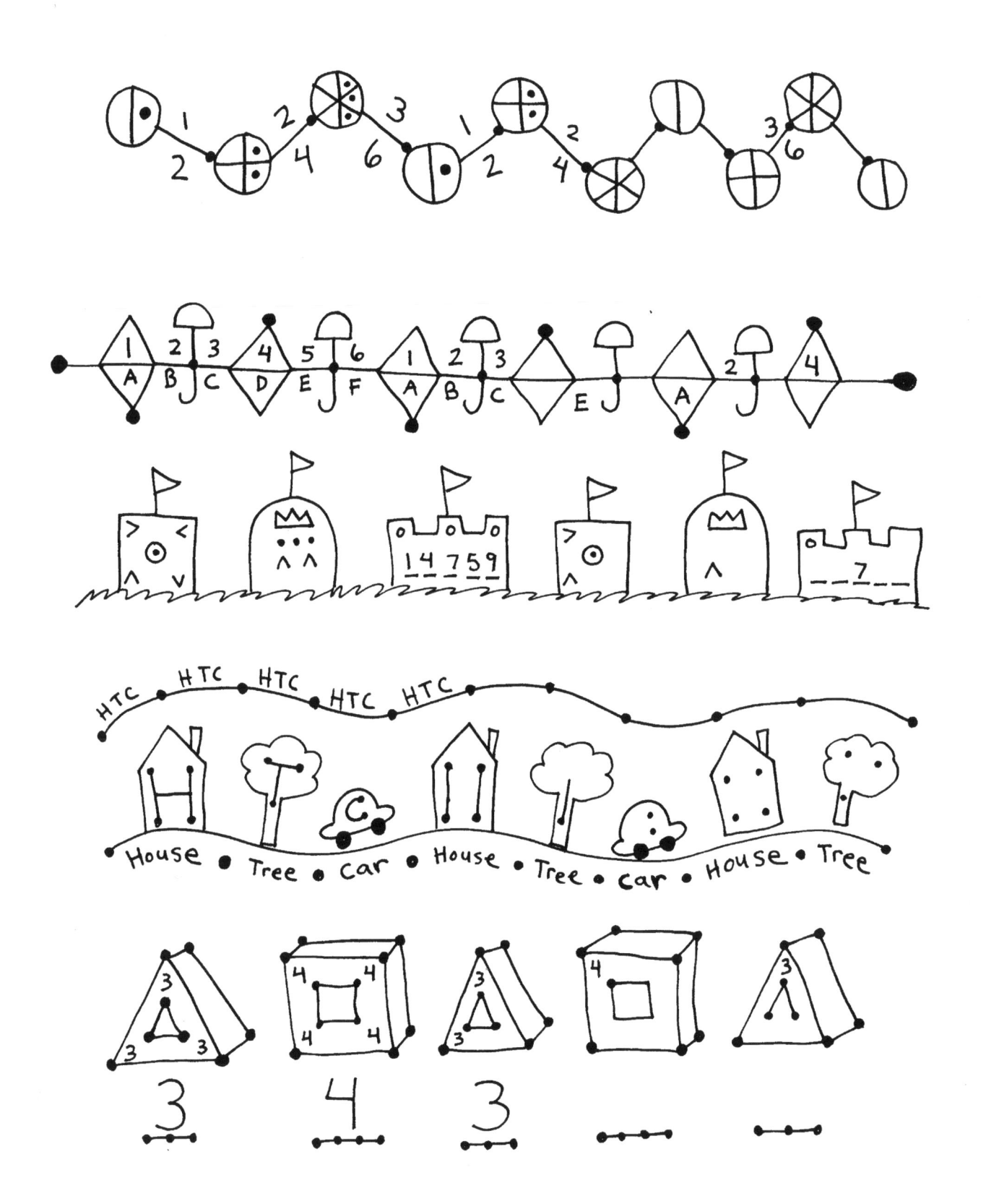

Name:_____ Date:_____

© 2011 all rights reserved. The Thinking Tree, LLC

Name:_____ Date:_____

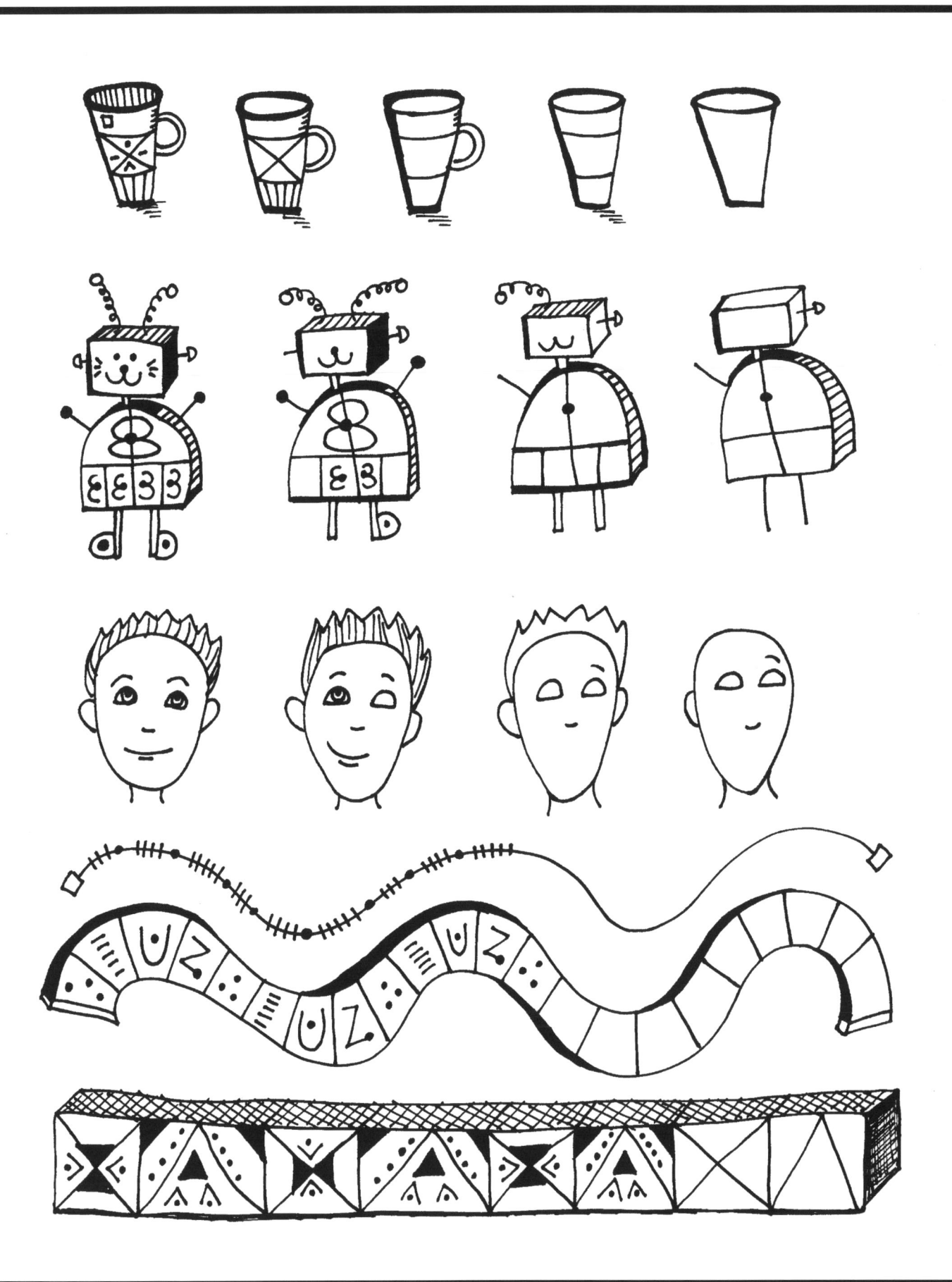

© 2011 all rights reserved. The Thinking Tree, LLC

A a E e I i A a

a e i a e i a e i

a e a e a

Name:_____ Date:_____

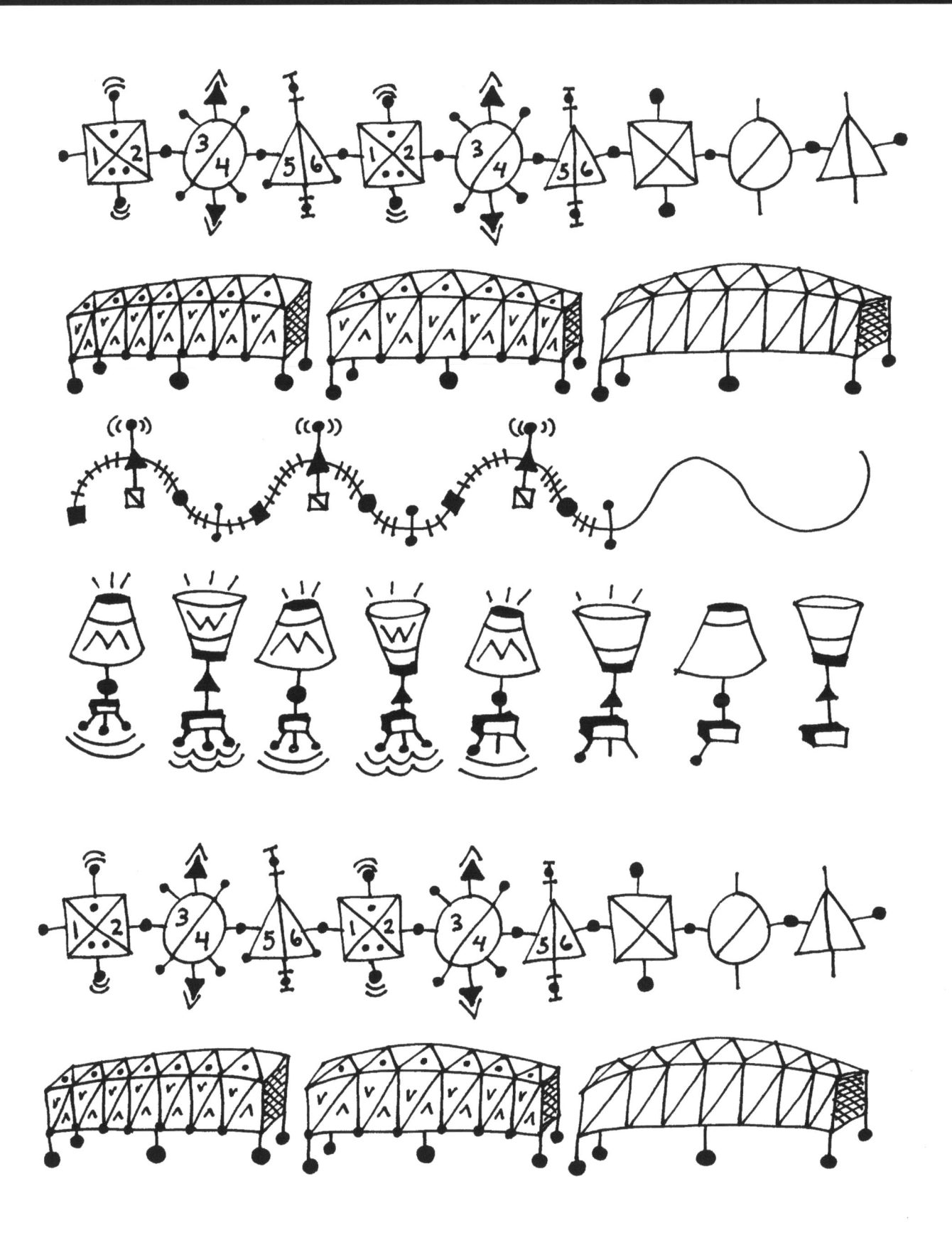

© 2011 all rights reserved. The Thinking Tree, LLC

Name:_____ Date:_____

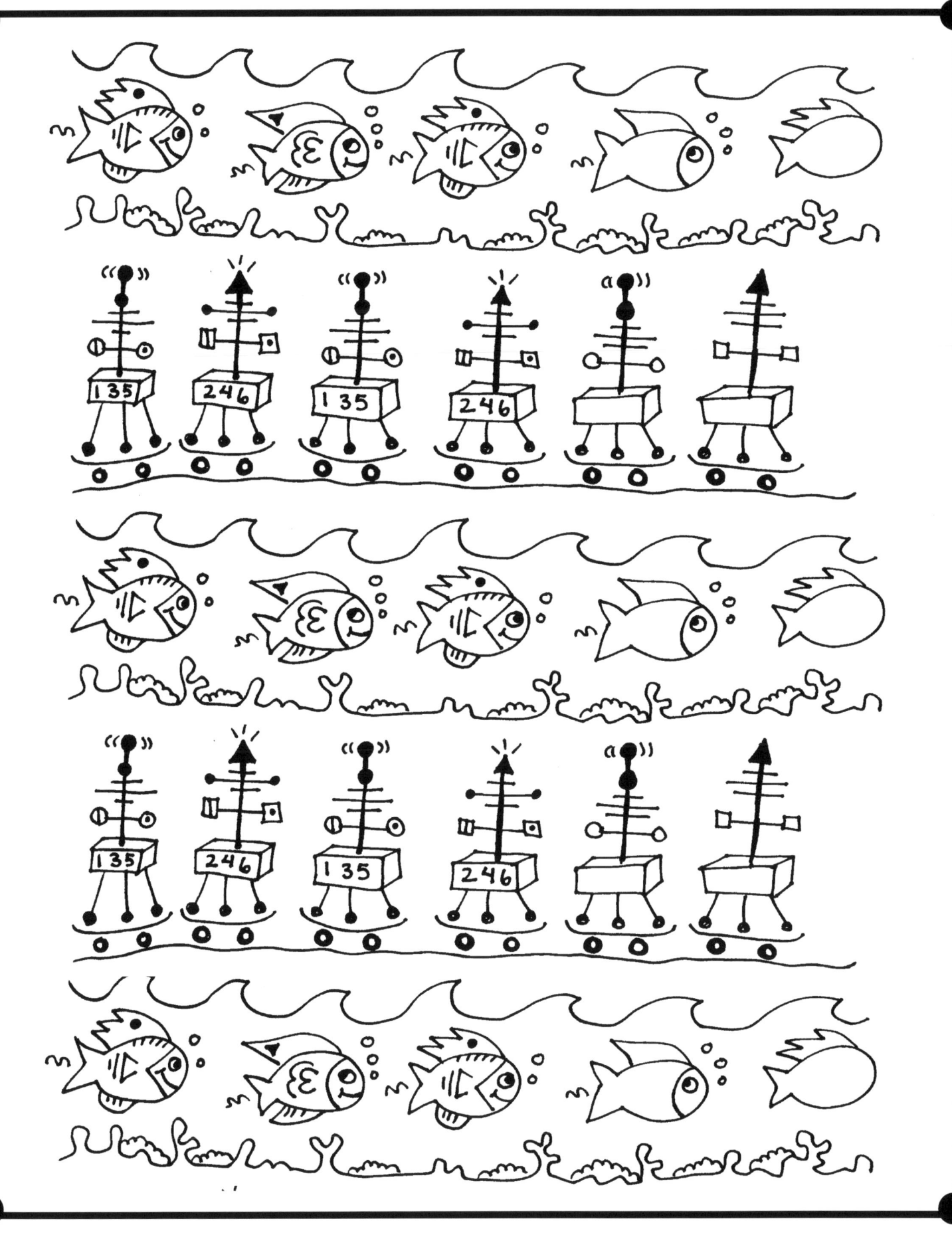

© 2011 all rights reserved. The Thinking Tree, LLC

Name:_____ Date:_____

BRAIN FOOD

Certificate of Completion

_____

Name & Age

_____

Date of Completion

The Thinking TREE

_____

Dyslexia Games

_____

Teacher

DyslexiaGames.com

BRAIN FOOD
Art Games, Puzzles & Patterns

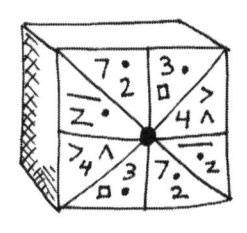

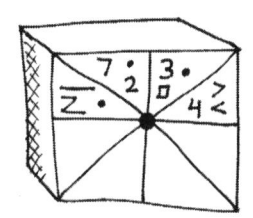

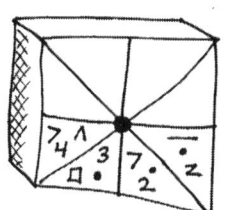

30 Lessons

"Finally, a fun solution for reading confusion!"

DyslexiaGames.com

Dyslexia Games Series A

- **ART FIRST** — 30 GAMES
- **Puzzling Patterns** — 30 GAMES
- **Letter Writing Games** — 30 GAMES
- **Draw & Spell** — 30 GAMES
- **Practice Pages** — 30 Worksheets
- **Word Hunt 1** — 30 Fun Games

Dyslexia Games Series B

- **BRAIN FOOD** — 30 Fun Lessons
- **I.Q. Challenge** — 30 GAMES
- **Practice Pages 2** — 30 Worksheets
- **Animal Art** — 30 Fun Lessons
- **Animal Talk** — 30 Fun Lessons
- **Word Hunt 2** — 30 Fun Games
- **Creative Copywork** — 45 Fun Lessons
- **Silly Animal Rhymes** — 30 RHYMES